DIRECTOR'S PLANNING GUIDE

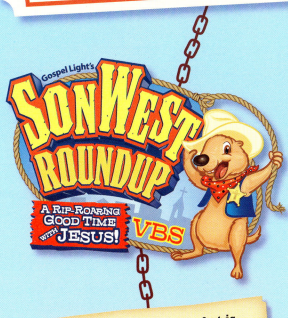

Gospel Light's
SonWest ROUNDUP
A RIP-ROARING GOOD TIME with JESUS! **VBS**

For a complete list of what is on the *Planning Guide CD-ROM*, see the Contents on pages 2-3. For a description of the files on the CD-ROM, read What's on It? in Folder B on the *Planning Guide CD-ROM*.

Folder A

The five major sections in this guide:

★ Director's Overview
★ Nursery & Toddler
★ Special Events
★ Step-by-Step Planning
★ Wild West Theme Guide

Folder B

All the articles at your fingertips, including:

★ Effective Training Meetings
★ First-Time Director Tips
★ Large Church Tips
★ Publicity Ideas
★ Safety First!
★ Small Church Tips
★ Using Youth Helpers

Folder C *

All the forms, checklists and newsletters, including:

★ Director's Checklist
★ Medical Release Form
★ Parent Newsletters
★ Publicity Checklist
★ SonWest Roundup Registration Form

Folder D *

Everything in this *Director's Planning Guide*—print, punch and put in a notebook!

* NOTE: Modifiable forms are located in Folder C only.

Check out all the resources available in the SonWest Digital Catalog on the *Planning Guide CD-ROM*.

Contents

Guidelines for Photocopying

Gospel Light Vacation Bible School

Publishing Director, Donna Lucas • **Senior Managing Editor,** Sheryl Haystead • **Associate Managing Editor,** Karen McGraw • **Editorial Team,** Anne Borghetti, Mary Gross Davis, Kristina Fucci, Janis Halverson • **Production Manager,** Peter Germann • **Art Director,** Lori Hamilton Redding • **Senior Designer,** Carolyn Thomas

Founder, Dr. Henrietta Mears • **Publisher,** William T. Greig • **Senior Consulting Publisher,** Dr. Elmer L. Towns • **Editorial Director, Biblical and Theological Content,** Dr. Gary S. Greig

Planning Guide CD-ROM

SonWest Digital Catalog

Folder A
Director's Overview (PDF of guide)
Nursery & Toddler (PDF of guide)
Special Events (PDF of guide)
Step-by-Step Planning (PDF of guide)
Wild West Theme Guide (PDF of guide)

Folder B
Activity Center Plan (PDF)
Asking Good Questions (PDF)
Backyard Bible School (PDF)

Building Relationships with Children (PDF)
Choose Your Format (PDF)
Choose Your Learning Plan (PDF)
Closing Program (PDF)
Dealing with Discipline (PDF)
Effective Training Meetings (PDF)
Family VBS (PDF)
First-Time Director's Tips (PDF)
Follow Up (PDF)
Get to Know the Countries (PDF)
Guidelines for Recruiting Success (PDF)
Large Church Tips (PDF)
Leading a Child to Christ (PDF)
Missionary Object Talks (PDF)
Missions & Service (PDF)
Missions Activities (PDF)
Planning Your Preschool VBS (PDF)
Playtime for Babies & Toddlers (PDF)
Prayer Team (PDF)
Preteen Enrichment Ideas (PDF)
Publicity Ideas (PDF)
Safety First! (PDF)
Service Project Ideas (PDF)
Small Church Tips (PDF)
Storytelling Techniques (PDF)
Theme Center Activities (PDF)
Understanding Religious Backgrounds (PDF)
Using Youth Helpers (PDF)
Volunteer List (PDF)
What's on It? (PDF)

Folder C

Activity Center Diagram (PDF)
Activity Center Plan for 36-48 First-Sixth Graders (PDF)
Activity Center Plan for 72-96 First-Sixth Graders (PDF)
Backyard Bible School Checklist (Modifiable PDF)
Backyard Bible School Schedule (Modifiable PDF)
Budget Worksheet (Modifiable PDF)
Closing Program Invitation (Modifiable PDF)
Course Overview Expanded *KJV* (Modifiable PDF)
Course Overview Expanded *NIV* (Modifiable PDF)
Course Overview *KJV* (PDF)

Course Overview *NIV* (PDF)
Direct Mail Flyer (Modifiable PDF)
Director's Checklist (Modifiable PDF)
Evening VBS Schedule (Modifiable PDF)
Family VBS Schedule Options (Modifiable PDF)
Follow-Up Invitation (Modifiable PDF)
How to Expand to a 10-Day VBS (PDF)
Injury Notification Form (Modifiable PDF)
Job Descriptions (Modifiable PDF)
Medical Release Form (Modifiable PDF)
News Release (Modifiable PDF)
Nursery Schedule (Modifiable PDF)
Parent Letter (Modifiable PDF)
Parent Newsletters (Modifiable PDF)
Parent Permission Form (Modifiable PDF)
Publicity Checklist (Modifiable PDF)
Recruitment Flyers (Modifiable PDF)
SonWest Roundup Invitation (Modifiable PDF)
SonWest Roundup Registration Form
    (Modifiable PDF)
SonWest Roundup Stationery (PDF)
VBS Questionnaire (PDF)
Volunteer Evaluation Form (Modifiable PDF)
Volunteer Newsletters (Modifiable PDF)
Wrangler Roundup Invitation (Modifiable PDF)
Wrangler Roundup Pass (Modifiable PDF)

Folder D

All the printed materials from Folders A, B and
C in this *Director's Planning Guide* arranged in
one file.

How to Use the Director's Planning Guide

As the VBS director, you have a wonderful opportunity to lead your volunteers in making a difference in kids' lives, helping kids discover how Jesus gives them what they need to overcome life's challenges. We've worked hard to give you the information you need in a way that makes it easy for you to prepare and lead. Follow the steps below to get the most out of your *Director's Planning Guide*.

Guidebook

Skim through this guide to get acquainted with the information in each section.

★ *Director's Overview* gives you a good idea of what SonWest Roundup is all about.

★ *Step-by-Step Planning* provides the key information you need to plan and organize your VBS.

★ *Wild West Theme Guide* is full of ways to make the theme come alive at your VBS!

★ *Special Events* is the perfect resource for making your Closing Program a success—and it includes plans for preview and Fall Kickoff events.

★ *Nursery & Toddler* features fun learning activities for little ones and guidelines for safe childcare.

> Use the "Director's Checklist" **C** to develop your own VBS to-do list.

Using the CD-ROM

Put the CD-ROM into your computer to see how it's organized. Having these files on a CD-ROM allows you to easily share information with the people who need it. You can either print out the information or send it via e-mail!

There are four folders on the CD-ROM:

★ **Folder A** contains the five main sections of this *Director's Planning Guide*.

★ **Folder B** contains all of the articles in alphabetical order.

★ **Folder C** contains all of the forms and newsletters.

★ **Folder D** contains everything in one document—just hit print, punch holes and place the whole thing in a three-ring binder!

Here are a few of the many ways you can use the files on the CD-ROM:

★ Use e-mail to send training articles to your leaders and helpers prior to training meetings. Then, during the meeting, review the information they read.

★ Print out the Job Descriptions in Folder C **C** and have them available to hand out when recruiting volunteers.

★ Instead of printing out the Volunteer Newsletters and Parent Newsletters, send them via e-mail!

★ See Volunteer List in Folder B **B** on the *Planning Guide CD-ROM* for more ideas of what to share with your leaders.

Now it's time to get started on the best VBS ever! Follow the easy directions in *Step-by-Step Planning*. Keep an eye out for the ▭ which means there is more information on the CD-ROM.

4

Where Can I Find . . . ?

Assembly Skit Scripts? . . . . *Rip-Roarin' Assemblies* book and CD-ROM
(includes modifiable files)

Bible Story Skit Scripts? . . . . *Rip-Roarin' Assemblies* book and CD-ROM
and in *Saddle Up! Bible Stories*

Clip Art (logos, patterns, stationery, etc.)? . . . *Wild West Décor & More CD-ROM*

Coloring Pages? . . . . *Wild West Décor & More* book and CD-ROM

Decorating Ideas? . . . . Overview DVD, *Wild West Décor & More* book and CD-ROM

Missionary Object Talks? . . . . Folder B **B** of the *Planning Guide CD-ROM*

Missions Project? . . . . Missions & Service in Folder B **B** of the
Planning Guide CD-ROM

Missions Center Activities? . . . . Missions Activities in Folder B **B** of the
Planning Guide CD-ROM

Music Center Activities? . . . . CD-ROM in the *Music Leader DVD & CD-ROM*

Music Videos? . . . . DVD in the *Music Leader DVD & CD-ROM*

Nursery & Toddler Curriculum? . . . . pages 34-40 in this guide and Folder A **A** of the
Planning Guide CD-ROM

Object Talks? . . . . Missionary Object Talks in Folder B **B** of the
Planning Guide CD-ROM

Piano Sheet Music? . . . . CD-ROM in the *Music Leader DVD & CD-ROM*

Promotional Skit Scripts? . . . . *Rip-Roarin' Assemblies* book and CD-ROM

Puppet Ideas for use with Preschoolers? . . . . *Pony Corral Teacher's Guide*

Service Project Ideas? . . . . Folder B **B** in the *Planning Guide CD-ROM*

Skit Videos? . . . . *Rip-Roarin' DVD*

Song PowerPoints? . . . . CD-ROM in the *Music Leader DVD & CD-ROM*
and *Rip-Roarin' Multimedia DVD*

Stationery? . . . . Folder C **C** in the *Planning Guide CD-ROM* (clip art to make
your own stationery is on the *Wild West Décor & More CD-ROM*)

Stunts for Assemblies? . . . . *Rip-Roarin' Assemblies* book and CD-ROM

Theme Center Activities? . . . . Folder B **B** in the *Planning Guide CD-ROM*

Word Charts for the songs? . . . . *Rip-Roarin' Multimedia DVD* and CD-ROM
in the *Music Leader DVD & CD-ROM*

Written descriptions of song motions? . . . . . . Download from gospellightvbs.com or myvbsparty.com

**For a full description of what is on the DVDs and CD-ROMs available for SonWest
Roundup, read What's on It? in Folder B B on the *Planning Guide CD-ROM*.**

DIRECTOR'S OVERVIEW

Saddle up your horses and get on over to SonWest Roundup!

Out in the wide-open spaces, we'll discover a colorful old town where all the excitement of the Wild West awaits! In SonWest, we'll celebrate all the fun of being buckaroos—so grab a sarsaparilla and join in the jamboree! There'll be food, games, music, crafts—and amazing true stories that point you and your kids to Jesus!

Ride with us under the deep blue skies. Feel the breezes rise through the shady purple canyons as we head out through this bright wilderness—we're traveling down the trail through the Old Testament stories of Moses to discover God's ultimate plan of salvation in Jesus, because "Jesus Christ is the same yesterday and today and forever" (Hebrews 13:8).

We dedicate this Gospel Light VBS to our Senior Managing Editor, a quiet hero of the faith, Sheryl Haystead (1951-2012). Her tireless devotion to produce curriculum materials that are true to God's Word and effective for children, as well as her passion for Jesus, continue to inspire us.

6

Course Description

In Session 1, we'll saddle up as God's **ULTIMATE PLAN** is revealed! We will discover that just as God had a plan to free the Israelites and sent Moses to rescue them from slavery in Egypt, He sent Jesus to rescue us from the slavery of sin. Kids will learn John 3:16, where Jesus describes God's astounding plan of salvation!

In Session 2, we'll giddy up to discover that **ULTIMATE POWER** is found in Jesus! We will discover that just as God showed His power to Moses at the burning bush, so He showed His mighty power to us through Jesus' life and miracles. In a world of big problems and huge crises, we'll find that Jesus' power is stronger than anything! Our Bible verse is John 16:33, where Jesus reminds us that He has overcome the world!

In Session 3, we'll ride out with the Israelites in the **ULTIMATE RESCUE**! We'll hear how God rescued His people from slavery in Egypt—even saving them from death! And we'll discover salvation and life forever with Jesus, made possible through His death and resurrection. The Bible verse is John 11:25, where Jesus tells that He is the resurrection and the life and that those who believe in Him will live forever with Him.

In Session 4, we will head up to explore **ULTIMATE TRUST**! We will learn how God provided for His people in the desert—and how Jesus provides for us every day, in every way! Kids will memorize John 6:35 and discover that we can trust Jesus to always provide what we need!

In Session 5, we'll round up to find **ULTIMATE LOVE**! As we hear about the time when Moses received God's commands at Mount Sinai, we will also discover that Jesus gave a new command. We'll see how loving Jesus means following His example and caring about others in our words and actions as He would. The Bible verse is John 13:34-35, Jesus' new commandment, given to His dearest friends—and to us.

So come on! Rustle up your kids and head on over to SonWest Roundup for a rip-roarin' good time!

SonWest Roundup

Bible Theme: Hebrews 13:8

Ultimate Point	Bible Story	Jesus Connection	Bible Verse
1 	**Born to Save** Exodus 1:1—2:10	**Preschool/Kindergarten** God sent Jesus because He has a plan for me! **Elementary** God cared about the Israelites and sent Moses to help them. God sent Jesus because He cares about me!	**Preschool/Kindergarten** "God so loved the world that he gave his one and only Son." John 3:16 **Elementary** "For God so loved the world that he gave his one and only Son, that whoever believes in him shall not perish but have eternal life." John 3:16
2 	**Promise of Power** Exodus 3:1—4:31	**Preschool/Kindergarten** Jesus has the power to help me—no matter what! **Elementary** God used His power to help Moses. Jesus' power is big enough to help me—no matter what!	**Preschool/Kindergarten** "When you have trouble, I will help you." (See John 16:33.) **Elementary** "In this world you will have trouble. But take heart! I have overcome the world." John 16:33
3 	**Passover Rescue** Exodus 5:1—12:51	**Preschool/Kindergarten** Jesus can rescue me from sin! **Elementary** God rescued the Israelites from slavery in Egypt. Jesus' death and resurrection can rescue me from sin and give me eternal life!	**Preschool/Kindergarten** "Anyone who believes in me will live." (See John 11:25.) **Elementary** "I am the resurrection and the life. He who believes in me will live, even though he dies." John 11:25
4 	**Perfect Provision** Exodus 16:1—17:7	**Preschool/Kindergarten** I can trust Jesus for what I need every day! **Elementary** The Israelites could trust God to provide for them. I can trust Jesus to take care of me every day!	**Preschool/Kindergarten** "Anyone who comes to me will never go hungry or be thirsty." (See John 6:35.) **Primary** "I am the bread of life. He who comes to me will never go hungry." John 6:35 **Middler/Preteen** "I am the bread of life. He who comes to me will never go hungry, and he who believes in me will never be thirsty." John 6:35
5	**Law of Love** Exodus 19:1—20:21; 24:12; 25:10-22	**Preschool/Kindergarten** I can be like Jesus and show love to others! **Elementary** God gave commands for the Israelites to follow. Jesus' new command is to follow Him and love others!	**Preschool/Kindergarten** "As I have loved you, so you must love one another." John 13:34 **Primary** "A new command I give you: Love one another. As I have loved you, so you must love one another." John 13:34 **Middler/Preteen** "A new command I give you: Love one another. As I have loved you, so you must love one another. By this all men will know that you are my disciples, if you love one another." John 13:34-35

Course Overview

Craft	Song	Snack	Recreation Game	Skit
Preschool Baby Moses in a Basket Frontier Vest **Younger Elementary** Moses' Basket Yarn-Art Box **Older Elementary** Rope & Wire Basket Manly Mustaches	"God Gave"	**Mud Bricks** Rice Krispies® treats are frosted with chocolate frosting and topped with graham-cracker crumbs. **Ropin' Rodeo Pasta** Pasta is tossed with butter or olive oil and Parmesan cheese.	**Preschool/Kindergarten** **Armadillos, Cross!** Children play a crawling version of Red Light, Green Light. **Elementary** **Pitchin' Party** Teams play a relay race where horseshoes, beanbags or other items are tossed into a hula-hoop target.	**That Dastardly Dirty Daryl** The good citizens of Dirt Clod are plumb tired of being bullied by that dastardly Dirty Daryl. Hank and Miss Lilly are at their wit's end trying to come up with a plan to save the town! Will no one come to rescue them?
Preschool Ribbon Snake Lizard Climber **Younger Elementary** Slither the Snake Bolo Tie **Older Elementary** T-Shirt Snake Beady Lizard	"Stronger Than Anything"	**Pretzel Staffs** Pretzel rods are dipped in frosting, covered with sprinkles and served with gummi "snakes." **Dusty Trail Fruit** Fruit chunks are dipped into a mixture of sour cream and brown sugar.	**Preschool/Kindergarten** **Lizard Warm Up** Children make guided motions to music. **Elementary** **Cowpoke Tag** Kids play a version of tag using "cowpokes" and "cattle."	**There's a New Sheriff in Town** At last the good folks of Dirt Clod have a hero on their side—Sheriff Otis Leroy Sunday! Sheriff Sunday has the power of the law and the governor on his side. But will that be enough power to rescue the citizens of Dirt Clod?
Preschool Puzzle Planks Stick Horse **Younger Elementary** Wooden Spool Cross Horse Sock Puppet **Older Elementary** Wooden Clothespin Cross Barbed Wire Cuff	"I Am the Resurrection"	**Passover Charoseth** Diced apples are mixed with cinnamon, raisins and honey. Served with saltine crackers. **Wagon-Wheel Cookies** Cookies are decorated with edible treats to look like wagon wheels.	**Preschool/Kindergarten** **Race to the Barn** Children form pairs to pretend to be a "horse" and "rider" and follow a trail. **Elementary** **Three-Legged Race** Teams compete in this classic game.	**In the Nick of Time** Dirty Daryl hatches a devious plot to drench Miss Lilly and Hank with a water bomb! Can they be rescued in time by Sheriff Sunday? What will this fiendish villain come up with next?
Preschool Cactus Flower Pot Moo-Zic Shaker **Younger Elementary** Leather Wallet Cowprint Cap **Older Elementary** Bird Bowl Wanted Poster	"He Will Provide"	**Mighty Manna** Popcorn is served with a variety of toppings for kids to choose from. **Cow Cupcakes** Cupcakes are decorated with cookies and candies to look like cow faces.	**Preschool/Kindergarten** **M-o-o-ve Along** Players use a broom or toy shovel to scoot a beanbag toward a goal. **Elementary** **Boulder Dash** Players try to avoid getting touched by a large "boulder" made from stuffing a large trash bag with newspaper.	**Showdown in Dirt Clod** In the dusty streets of Dirt Clod, Dirty Daryl and Sheriff Sunday have a thrilling showdown. Will good triumph over evil? Can the folks of Dirt Clod really trust Sheriff Sunday to provide for and protect them? Or will Dirty Daryl prevail?
Preschool My Book of 10 Prairie-Dog Plant Stake **Younger Elementary** Message Board Prairie Dog Tag **Older Elementary** Bible Book Cover Mason Jar Lantern	"The Way We Love"	**Waffle Tablets** Waffles are trimmed to look like tablets and topped with fruit jelly, fruit slices, syrup or whipped cream. **Prairie Dog Burrows** Hot dogs and cheese are wrapped in dough and baked.	**Preschool/Kindergarten** **Prairie Dog Popup** Children play a game where they follow instructions to form different kinds of groups. **Elementary** **Cattle Driver's Obstacle Course** Teams run an obstacle-course race using skills they might use on a cattle drive.	**Ridin' Off into the Sunset** Now that Dirty Daryl has been locked up, Sheriff Sunday declares it's time to move on down the trail. But before he goes, he needs deputies to continue the loving good deeds he began. Who can fill the big boots of Sheriff Sunday?

Super Starter Kit

This kit provides all you'll need for the best VBS ever.
The Super Starter Kit includes all of these items (described below):

★ **Starter Kit**   ★ **Director's Sample Pack**   ★ **Additional Resources**

Starter Kit

Your Starter Kit contains samples of materials that have been carefully designed to help you promote and conduct an effective SonWest Roundup VBS. Each Starter Kit includes the following:

★ *Director's Planning Guide*

★ *Overview DVD* The preview segment on this DVD will give you a quick overview that you can use to introduce the various facets of your VBS to your volunteers, congregation, etc. Also included on the DVD are video clips of Bible teaching; decorating ideas; crafts, games and snacks; music clips; plus, information about the large group assembly and The Pony Corral (VBS for preschoolers).

★ *Saddle Up! Bible Stories* These age-level teaching manuals contain what every leader needs to tell the Bible stories and lead life-application activities.

★ *Pony Corral Teacher's Guide* This is a teaching manual for the teachers of children who are ages three to six. It contains all the information and reproducible pages needed to lead stories, activities, games and snacks for these self-contained classrooms.

★ *Preschool Fun Pages & Elementary Student Guides* These colorful keepsakes are must-have VBS souvenirs! They are filled with Bible story reviews and fun, life-application activities. These fun pages and student guides are available for all age levels and are a tool teachers can use to make sure essential Bible truths are understood by children. Taken home, they help parents know what was learned and how to reinforce that learning.

★ *Rodeo Ring Bible Games* This teaching manual for the Bible Games Center provides all the information and reproducible resources needed to lead children in creative, theme-related games. For each session there are two games: one to review the Bible story and the other to review the Bible verse.

★ *Trading Post Crafts for Kids* This book contains 30 great craft ideas using readily available materials. There is a specific project in the craft book for every age and every session (see SonWest Roundup Course Overview, pp. 8-9). Includes CD-ROM.

★ **Director's Sample Pack** See description on the next page.

Keep this handy list as a guide to all your SonWest Roundup products.

10

Director's Sample Pack

This pack includes a sample of the following:

⭐ **Volunteer Pocket Guide** This handy booklet helps train members of your VBS team and contains each day's Bible story, Bible verse, Jesus Connection and discussion questions as well as a place for volunteers to record the essential information that they need.

⭐ **Parent Pocket Guide** Similar to the *Volunteer Pocket Guide*, this booklet contains each day's Bible story, Bible verse, Jesus Connection, a parent devotional and discussion questions to keep parents informed of all their children are learning at SonWest Roundup. Also included are suggestions for fun family activities.

⭐ **Attendance Chart** This colorful chart can be used to record children's attendance or Bible verse memorization.

⭐ **Bookmark** Give away bookmarks as awards and prizes.

⭐ **Bulletin Cover/Insert or Publicity Flyer** These full-color 8½x11-inch (21.5x28-cm) sheets may be printed with your information on the back. Fold in half to use as bulletin covers, or cut apart to use as bulletin inserts or publicity flyers.

⭐ **Doorknob Hanger** Hang these colorful invitations to SonWest Roundup VBS on the houses near your church.

⭐ **Iron-On T-Shirt Transfer** Use this colorful design to identify VBS team members or to give every child a personal SonWest Roundup memento.

⭐ **Magnet** Send one of these magnets home with every child and volunteer.

⭐ **Name Tag** Use these VBS name tags for each team member, child and visitor.

⭐ **Photo Frame** These frames make great thank-you items for team members and are ideal for following up with children.

⭐ **Postcard** Mail these full-color postcards to invite children to VBS.

⭐ **Publicity Poster** Advertise your VBS in the community with these beautiful posters.

⭐ **Skin Decals** These colorful skin transfers feature the Ultimate Points.

⭐ **SonWest Stickers** These colorful stickers are perfect for crafts, awards and charting children's attendance.

⭐ **Student Certificate** Give these colorful certificates at the end of VBS.

⭐ **Volunteer Certificate** Recognize and thank the members of your VBS team with this certificate.

⭐ **Evangelism and Discipling Booklets** *God Loves You!* and *Following Jesus* will help you talk with children about becoming members of God's family and learning to live as His children.

⭐ **And More!**

Additional Resources

Essential resources for activity leaders, exciting decorating helps and everything you need to lead music, stage skits and present the Closing Program.

⭐ ***Miss Sheryl's Snack Cards*** Everything a leader needs to provide a variety of Bible story or theme-related snacks. Includes a daily Talk Time card to spark discussions at the snack table!

⭐ ***Giddy Up! Game Cards*** Everything a leader needs to provide a variety of theme-related recreation games.

⭐ ***Poster Packs*** These colorful resources are filled with ideas and materials to enhance Bible learning. The *Pony Corral Posters & Props* contains a Bible story big book for each session, Stand-up Activity cards, Bible verse posters and decorating posters designed for preschool and kindergarten classrooms. The *Bible Teaching Poster Pack* contains Bible verse posters and Bible story posters for elementary classrooms. The *Decorating Poster Pack* contains decorating posters for all areas of your VBS.

⭐ ***Wild West Décor & More*** This book contains a wealth of decorating ideas and patterns, clip art, coloring pages and more! Includes CD-ROM.

⭐ **Ultimate Point Pennants** Use these colorful signs to designate classrooms and to identify groups.

⭐ ***Music & More CD*** This reproducible CD contains both full-mix and split-track recordings for six songs. Two preschool songs are also included. This CD also includes sound effects for the Bible stories and the Assembly skits! Make copies of this CD for your children to take home or purchase *Student Music Packs*.

> Instead of duplicating the SonWest Roundup music for all your VBS children and team members, you may purchase *Student Music Packs* of 10 CDs. These CDs contain all of the SonWest Roundup songs.

⭐ ***Music Leader DVD & CD-ROM*** SonWest Roundup songs make Scripture truths come alive for singers and listeners alike. The DVD provides music videos as well as instructional videos to teach the motions. The CD-ROM contains piano sheets with guitar chord notations, Music Center activities for each session and song PowerPoints. (Note: Written descriptions for the steps and motions are available as a download at our websites, gospellightvbs.com and myvbsparty.com.)

⭐ ***Rip-Roarin' Assemblies*** This reproducible book includes opening and closing assembly helps, assembly stunts and skit scripts, a promotional skit, Bible story skits, tips for producing puppet skits and a script and instructions for planning the Closing Program. Also included are patterns and directions for making backdrops, props and set pieces. Includes CD-ROM.

⭐ ***Rip-Roarin' Multimedia CD-ROM*** NEW! On this CD-ROM you will find cool resources to pump up your opening or closing assemblies. Included are the SonWest Roundup logo, daily logos, Bible story posters, Bible verse posters and song PowerPoints. Simply pop this CD-ROM in your computer and upload the files to your presentation software.

⭐ ***Rip-Roarin' DVD*** This DVD has everything you need to show fun skits during VBS on one handy DVD. Show the assembly skits on this DVD as a rehearsal help for your live skits or during your VBS in place of live skit presentations. The Cowboy Cool videos, which feature the daily animals, can be shown during assemblies, snack time, while waiting for parents to pick up kids or any time you have children assembled in one place. Also on this DVD is the missions video featuring the One Million Children project through Gospel Light Worldwide.

⭐ **And More!**

Gospel Light Ordering Guide

To help you decide what and how much to order, follow these steps.

STEP 1

Decide the centers you will offer. **Tip:** Plan a maximum of 24 to 36 children in a center at a time.

STEP 2

List the number of teachers you will have for each center. **Tip:** One teacher for every eight children with a minimum of two teachers for every center.

STEP 3

Order

- ★ **Director:** In addition to the *Director's Planning Guide*, order *Wild West Décor & More*

- ★ **Guides, Helpers or Assistants:** *Volunteer Pocket Guide* (one for each)

- ★ **Bible Story Leaders or Teachers:**
  - *Saddle Up! Bible Stories* • *Grades 1 and 2* and *Bible Teaching Poster Pack*
  - *Saddle Up! Bible Stories* • *Grades 3 and 4* (Use this center guide if you combine ages) and *Bible Teaching Poster Pack*
  - *Saddle Up! Bible Stories* • *Grades 5 and 6* and *Bible Teaching Poster Pack*

- ★ **Preschool Leader:** *Pony Corral Teacher's Guide* and *Pony Corral Posters & Props*

- ★ **Kids:**
  - Preschool/Kindergarten: *Pony Corral Fun Pages* (one for each child)
  - Grades 1 and 2, *Head 'Em Out!* student guide (one for each child)
  - Grades 3 and 4, *Move 'Em Out!* student guide (one for each child)
  - Grades 5 and 6, *Ridin' Out* student guide (one for each child)

- ★ **Assembly Leader:** *Rip-Roarin' Assemblies*, *Rip-Roarin' Multimedia CD-ROM* and *Rip-Roarin' DVD*

- ★ **Music Leader:** *Music Leader DVD & CD-ROM* and *Music & More CD*

- ★ **Snack Leader:** *Miss Sheryl's Snack Cards*

- ★ **Recreation Leader:** *Giddy Up! Game Cards*

- ★ **Craft Leader:** *Trading Post Crafts for Kids*

- ★ **Bible Games Leader:** *Rodeo Ring Bible Games* and *Bible Teaching Poster Pack*

Ordering Note: If children remain in one classroom for all activities instead of rotating from center to center, order one of these items for each elementary classroom teacher: appropriate age-level *Saddle Up! Bible Stories*, *Bible Teaching Poster Pack* and the guides for other activities (crafts, Bible games, etc.). For each preschool classroom teacher, order *Pony Corral Teacher's Guide* and *Pony Corral Posters & Props*.

STEP-BY-STEP PLANNING

Step 1: Plan

The steps outlined here are the key tasks that need to be accomplished to fulfill your job as VBS director. As you work through these bite-sized steps, you may want to use the Director's Checklist **C** to create your own VBS to-do list.

Get going on your best VBS ever by establishing the basics of your VBS.

★ **Choose Your Format.** **B** While a 5-day program is still the most common choice for VBS, there are other options to consider—weekend, Family VBS **B**, Backyard Bible School **B**, all-summer, etc. Consider the availability of teachers, facilities and the number of children in daycare and then choose what will work best for your church.

★ **Choose Your Date and Time.** Consult with other children's ministry leaders at your church and check the church master calendar. Consider school schedules, summer camp dates, popular vacation times for children and families and then choose the date and time that will work best for your church.

★ **Choose Your Learning Plan.** **B** The learning plan is the schedule of what you're going to teach and when you're going to teach it. Most churches use the activity center plan because leaders prepare and present only one specific activity each day. Other options are classroom-based and site-based learning plans.

★ **Create the Daily Schedule.** Estimate how many groups of kids you will have (up to 24 in a group) and determine which rooms are available in your facility. (Confirm rooms with your church's master calendar.) Then use the Activity Center Plan **B** to create a master schedule.

★ **Plan Your Budget.** Use the Budget Worksheet **C** to help you estimate your expenses and list sources of income.

★ **Order Curriculum.** Now that you have your plans in place, order curriculum materials for all center leaders, preschool teachers and children. Use last year's attendance reports as a guide. For more information on ordering see Ordering Guide on page 13.

When you see a **B**, there is an article with more information and details in Folder B on the *Planning Guide CD-ROM*. When you see a **C**, a form, checklist, flyer or newsletter is in Folder C on the CD-ROM.

Activity Center Diagram

Opening/Closing Assembly

Bible Story Center

Choose one or more. *

Music Center

Bible Games Center

Theme Center

Craft Center

Missions and Service Center

Recreation and Snack Center

* You may choose to replace Snacks, Recreation Games, Crafts or Music with one of these centers.

Need More Help? Look in Folder B **B** on the *Planning Guide CD-ROM* for these articles: First-Time Director Tips, Large Church Tips, Planning Your Preschool VBS, Prayer Team, Preteen Enrichment Ideas, Small Church Tips and Safety First!

Step 2: Recruit

VBS is an excellent opportunity for many people to discover, use and develop their gifts—and make an eternal impact in the lives of children. So as you recruit, don't forget to inspire and communicate the vision of VBS! Here's what to do.

⭐ **Determine Staffing Needs.** Make a Volunteer List **B** of all the jobs that need to be done, no matter how small. Some tasks can be combined to be done by one person. Then estimate the total number of volunteers you will need, using these recommended team-member-to-student ratios: 1 adult for every 6 preschoolers; 1 adult for every 8 grade-school children; minimum of 2 adults in each classroom.

⭐ **Determine Job Tasks.** Write a brief Job Description **C** of the tasks for each job so that your volunteers know what is expected of them.

⭐ **List Potential Volunteers.** Pray for guidance (and get a prayer partner or two) and list potential volunteers. Include former VBS volunteers, youth, parents, college students and senior citizens.

⭐ **Contact and Follow Up with Potential Volunteers.** Create a Recruitment Flyer **C** . Send the flyer to all potential volunteers. Then follow up with personal e-mails or phone calls to answer questions and let them know what curriculum and training you will provide them.

⭐ **Display a Sign-Up Poster.** Many churches will display a volunteer sign-up poster in a well-traveled place. Update it each week and feature fun Western animals and/or photos. (A tasty snack guarantees lots of visitors to your sign-up table!)

Need More Help? Look in Folder B **B** on the CD-ROM for these articles: Guidelines for Recruiting Success and Using Youth Helpers.

Elementary Coordinator

Date and Time: June 18-22 from 9:00 to 12:00

Resources Available
- ☐ *Saddle Up! Bible Stories* for each age level: Grades 1 and 2, Grades 3 and 4, Grades 5 and 6
- ☐ Center guides as needed for additional centers such as crafts, snacks, Bible games, etc.

Responsibilities
- ☐ Supervise age-level activities for children ages 6 to 12

Elementary Age-Level Teachers

Date and Time: June 18-22 from 9:00 to 12:00

Resources Available
- ☐ *Saddle Up! Bible Stories*
- ☐ Bible Teaching Poster Pack
- ☐ Student guides—one for each child
- ☐ Rodeo Ring Bible Games
- ☐ Trading Post Crafts for Kids
- ☐ Theme Center Activities (in Folder B **B** on the Planning Guide CD-ROM)
- ☐ Miss Sheryl's Snack Cards
- ☐ Giddy Up! Game Cards

If teacher is also teaching music, he or she will need
- ☐ Music Leader DVD & CD-ROM
- ☐ Music & More CD

Optional:
- ☐ Brief, written description of motions (available as a download at gospellightvbs.com)

(Modify resources as needed according to the time available.)

Responsibilities
- ☐ Plan and present the entire lesson (Bible story, games, crafts, etc.) to a class in one classroom
- ☐ Gather and prepare lesson materials
- ☐ Be prepared to use the suggested conversation to help children review each day's Bible story and Bible verse and apply them to their lives

VACATION BIBLE SCHOOL VOLUNTEERS

Dates _____

Time _____

I would like to help in one or more of the following areas (please circle):

Decorating	Bible teaching	Music	Special events
Prayer support	Crafts	Skits	Follow-up
Publicity	Group guide	Snacks	Youth helper
Missions project	Recreation games		

Other _____

Name _____

Address _____

Phone (home) _____

Phone (cell) _____

E-mail _____

If you have any questions about Vacation Bible School or your involvement in it, please call

_____
(name and phone number)

PLEASE RETURN THIS FLYER IN THE OFFERING PLATE OR TO THE CHURCH OFFICE.

Step 3: Train

Beginnings are the most important times for new volunteers, so make every effort to train and prepare your volunteers. We've provided the keys to successful training below.

★ **Plan a General Training Meeting.** Whether your church is large or small, every church needs to plan a general meeting at least a month before VBS begins. Large churches may also ask age-level leaders to schedule a planning meeting for team members several weeks before VBS. (See Effective Training Meetings **B** .)

★ **Determine Additional Training Needs.** Some churches also conduct meetings or distribute training articles related to specific topics such as these which are all found in Folder B **B** on the *Planning Guide CD-ROM*: Asking Good Questions, Building Relationships with Children, Dealing with Discipline, Storytelling Techniques and Understanding Religious Backgrounds.

★ **Prepare for Training Meetings.** Follow these tips:

- Schedule each meeting at a time you think most volunteers will be able to attend.
- Reserve the date(s) on the church calendar.
- Use the church bulletin or website, e-mails, postcards and/or phone calls to let volunteers know the meeting date(s) and time(s).
- Create an agenda for your meeting. Look at the Effective Training Meetings article **B** for sample agendas. Be sure to cover the importance of evangelism (see p. 19).
- List and collect the supplies you need.

> **Build relationships with your volunteer team by starting your meeting with one of these ice breakers: Ask volunteers to tell which is their favorite Western movie and why. Or, have each person share a favorite memory from a trip to a Wild-West town.**

Step 4: Publicize

The goal of your publicity is to communicate that VBS is a "Can't Miss This!" experience. Well-planned publicity is critical to the success of VBS. Whether you take charge of publicity yourself or you have a Publicity Coordinator, follow these steps and use these tools.

★ **List Publicity Ideas.** Referring to Publicity Ideas **B**, make a list of all the publicity options you have available: church bulletin/newsletters, e-mails, online social networking sites, text messages, outdoor banners, flyers, posters, etc. Gospel Light provides a variety of items you can purchase (look at the samples in the Director's Sample Pack or check out the SonWest Digital Catalog on the *Planning Guide CD-ROM* or gospellightvbs.com).

★ **Plan Your Publicity.** Select the ideas you think will work best and what you can afford. Make sure your plan includes several ways to build interest within your church and also ideas for reaching out to children from the community.

★ **Make a Publicity Schedule.** Now it's time to plan the schedule. What's the key? Start early! Begin with a save-the-date notice before family calendars get filled up. Use the Publicity Checklist **C** to help you stay on track.

★ **Create Publicity Materials.** **C** Have fun creating your publicity items! Get a head start by using the Direct Mail Flyer, News Release and Invitations (Wrangler Roundup, SonWest Roundup, Closing Program and Follow Up) we've provided for you in Folder C **C**!

> **Grab attention for your VBS by holding a preview event a week or two before VBS begins. Invite kids and parents for an hour or two of games, refreshments, crafts, skits and other fun activities. Read about Wrangler Roundup in Special Events (p. 31) and also in Folder A **A** of the *Planning Guide CD-ROM* for information to help you plan a preview event.**

> **Need More Help?** There is a sample SonWest Roundup Registration Form in Folder C **C** on the CD-ROM.

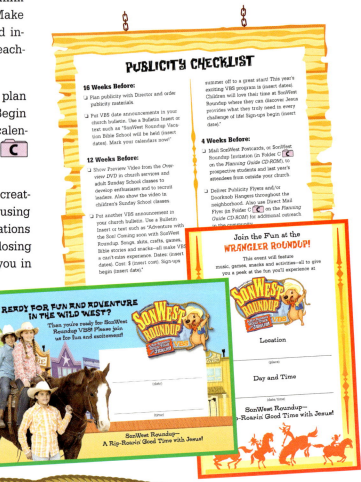

PUBLICITY CHECKLIST

16 Weeks Before:

☐ Plan publicity with Director and order publicity materials.

☐ Put VBS date announcements in your church bulletin. Use a Bulletin Insert or text such as "SonWest Roundup Vacation Bible School will be held (insert dates). Mark your calendars now!"

12 Weeks Before:

☐ Show Preview Video from the *Overview DVD* in church services and adult Sunday School classes to develop enthusiasm and to recruit leaders. Also show the video in children's Sunday School classes.

☐ Put another VBS announcement in your church bulletin. Use a Bulletin Insert or text such as "Adventure with the Son! Coming soon with SonWest Roundup. Songs, skits, crafts, games, Bible stories and snacks—all make VBS a can't-miss experience. Dates: (insert dates). Cost: $ (insert cost). Sign-ups begin (insert date)."

summer off to a great start! This year's exciting VBS program is (insert dates). Children will love their time at SonWest Roundup where they can discover Jesus provides what they truly need in every challenge of life! Sign-ups begin (insert date)."

4 Weeks Before:

☐ Mail SonWest Postcards, or SonWest Roundup Invitation (in Folder C **C** on the *Planning Guide CD-ROM*), to prospective students and last year's attendees from outside your church.

☐ Deliver Publicity Flyers and/or Doorknob Hangers throughout the neighborhood. Also use Direct Mail Flyer (in Folder C **C** on the *Planning Guide CD-ROM*) for additional outreach in the community.

Join the Fun at the WRANGLER ROUNDUP!

This event will feature music, games, snacks and activities—all to give you a peek at the fun you'll experience at

READY FOR FUN AND ADVENTURE IN THE WILD WEST?

Then you're ready for SonWest Roundup VBS! Please join us for fun and excitement!

SonWest Roundup—A Rip-Roarin' Good Time with Jesus!

Location
(place)

Day and Time
(date/time)

SonWest Roundup—A Rip-Roarin' Good Time with Jesus!

Step 5: Evangelize

SonWest Roundup VBS presents a unique opportunity to share the gospel with children and their families. With all the planning that takes place for VBS crafts, games, music and more, don't forget to plan for the heart of VBS—reaching kids for Jesus.

To ensure your team is prepared for evangelism, take time during your training meeting to do the following:

- ⭐ **Know the Lesson Conclusion.** So that the gospel message can be given in every lesson, point out to teachers that the Conclusion in each day's Bible story helps them know what to say to talk with children about becoming Christians.

- ⭐ **Prepare Personal Testimonies.** So that volunteers are prepared to talk with children about salvation, ask each one to write three to five sentences, using words that kids will understand, about how they decided to follow Jesus. Talk about using words and phrases that children will understand.

- ⭐ **Share Resources.** Give team members evangelism resources (Leading a Child to Christ **B** , *God Loves You!* and *Following Jesus*) to use with children. Suggest teachers use the *God Loves You!* booklet in Sessions 2, 3 or 4 and *Following Jesus* booklet in Session 5.

- ⭐ **Use Assembly Time.** During assemblies and/or the Closing Program, provide opportunities for youth and adult helpers to share why they decided to follow Jesus.

Ask each adult small group in your church to pray for the salvation and Christian growth of children in a specific VBS class. You may wish to provide these prayer partners with the names of children for whom to pray.

God Loves You! and *Following Jesus* are booklets available from Gospel Light that you can use with kids at VBS—and send home for parents to use, too. *God Loves You!* helps children understand what the Bible says about salvation and how to become a Christian. *Following Jesus* gives kids who are new believers practical tips on ways they can grow to become disciples of Jesus.

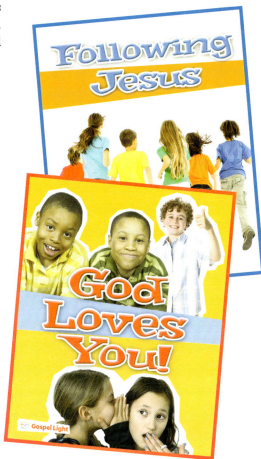

Be ready to maximize the full potential of your VBS by planning a proactive follow-up program. You can continue the impact of SonWest Roundup in a variety of ways. Ready for MORE fun?

★ **Follow Up on Children and Families.** There are three basic ways to build on the momentum of VBS:

- Take advantage of what your curriculum offers you and make sure that the SonWest Roundup student resources—Preschool/Kindergarten *Pony Corral Fun Pages* and Elementary student guides—are sent home with children. These cool, kid-appealing resources will help kids and parents know more about Jesus.

- You can also plan one or more children's or family activities in the months following VBS. Mail a flyer to all your church and VBS families. Anyone for pizza in the park?

- Kick off your fall programs with an invitation to each unchurched VBS family. You might even enclose a DVD of fun VBS activities as a reminder of your church's wonderful children's programs. Even better, plan a Fall Kickoff event using ideas from Wrangler Roundup on page 31.

> **Need More Help?** Read Follow Up Ideas in Folder B **[B]** on the CD-ROM for a treasure trove of practical ideas.

Keep the spirit of VBS alive all summer with the curriculum designed to go along with SonWest Roundup: Gospel Light's *Wrangler Roundup*, a 13-lesson adventure for children ages 3-12. The fun and excitement of your own Wild-West town is combined with the discovery of the ULTIMATE gifts Jesus provides for members of God's family.

★ **Follow Up with Your Staff.** Plan at least one way to say "thank you" to all your team members. A small gift, a thank-you note or a certificate can show your appreciation. Also, ask team members to complete a Volunteer Evaluation Form **[C]** with suggestions for improvement.

★ **Follow Up on Administrative Issues.** While the events of VBS are still fresh in your mind, compile and file all records, receipts, checklists, personnel lists and publications. Write down your ideas for next year's program.

★ **Follow Up in Your Church.** Many people in your church will want to know the results of their support and prayer—and they are all potential volunteers for next year! So plan a way for a few VBS kids and leaders to share their response to the week (newsletter article, interview during church event, etc.) and/or plan a visual display of VBS activities (video, photo display, etc.).

★ **And Don't Forget Yourself!** Plan a way to refresh your body and soul. Praise God for His strength and provision.

> **You can complete the VBS Questionnaire online at www.gospellight.com/vbssurvey. Or fill out and submit the VBS Questionnaire in Folder C [C].**

WILD WEST THEME GUIDE

A Western town is wild and exciting and FUN! Kids love the thrilling adventure of life in a Western town! Make your VBS the best ever by using these ideas to make the Wild West come to life for your VBS kids.

⭐ Add an unforgettable dimension to your VBS by filling your church with the Sights & Sounds of SonWest Roundup (below).

⭐ Use our suggestions to enhance the fun for your kids, or "Cowpokes" (pp. 23-24).

⭐ Your VBS team will love these extra-fun ideas developed just for them in "Wild-West Workers" (p. 25).

For even more ideas shared by VBS directors from all over, visit the discussion forums at gospellightvbs.com, myvbsparty.com, the Gospel Light Facebook page and the SonWest Roundup Pinterest boards.

Sights & Sounds

Scenery

Add paper to walls and paint them to look like a Wild-West landscape: cactus, mountains, brush, etc. Use the patterns and ideas in *Wild West Décor & More* and the Decorating Ideas segments of the *Overview DVD* to decorate your classrooms and activity centers. Clip art is available in *Wild West Décor & More* and at gospellightvbs.com.

Decorating Contest

Every year, hold a decorating contest. Give a prize to the room with the most exciting decorations. Or, instead of one prize, give a variety of prizes: Best Door, Best Ceiling, Best Hallway, etc. Find something special about every room so that each room receives a prize!

Enter In

Plan a cool entrance. Construct a large sign painted with the words "SonWest Roundup" on it. Make it large enough to span the entrance to your church parking lot and suspend it from trees or on tall poles. Turn your light poles into cacti by wrapping the poles with green paper and attaching green pool noodles for the arms of the cactus. Set up inflatable cactus or inflatable "wooden" fencing to line the walkways leading to your Welcome Center or assembly room. Look for patterns in *Wild West Décor & More* to make your entrances one-of-a-kind!

SonWest Town Square

What's in a Name?

Give your rooms or centers names appropriate for your VBS. We suggest the following: SonWest Town Square (Assembly Room) for opening and closing assemblies, Miss Sheryl's Snack Parlor for snacks, Trading Post for crafts, Golden Saddle Theater for Bible Story Center, Rodeo Ring for Bible Games. (See *Wild West Décor & More* for sketches and instructions for decorating all the suggested rooms.) Feel free to make up your own names to suit your facility.

Rounding Up Roundup Supplies

Write down supplies and materials needed for VBS on theme-related die-cuts, such as cactus, horse or cow shapes. Place die-cuts in a basket for church members to choose. On a large sheet of butcher paper, draw a landscape with mountains in the background and a sun in the sky. Post landscape on a wall near the VBS information table. After church members choose a die-cut, they purchase or donate the needed item and then tape die-cut to landscape you prepared. A bulletin announcement will invite church members to "Be a Part of SonWest Roundup!"

Transitions

To signal transition times in your schedule, consider the following ideas:

⭐ Through your church sound system, play "SonWest Roundup" from *Music & More CD*.

⭐ Blow an air horn.

⭐ Ask a volunteer to dress like a cowboy, Western animal or as your VBS mascot (see VBS Mascot on p. 25) and walk throughout your campus, ringing a cowbell, blowing a whistle or speaking through a megaphone.

Music, Music, Music

Make your VBS come to life using sounds. The *Music & More CD* provides lively songs to enhance your atmosphere and to help VBS children learn Bible truths to help them discover great things about Jesus. You can also purchase CDs that have instrumental versions of Western songs. Play the songs as kids gather for VBS to begin and while kids are waiting to be picked up, in classrooms during activities, hallways during transitions, etc. Don't confine the music to indoor areas, but set up speakers outside as well.

How Far?

In a central area, such as where classes gather for assemblies or in the snack center, post pictures of different famous western towns (Tombstone, Arizona; Dodge City, Kansas; Abilene, Texas; Deadwood, South Dakota; etc.). Under each picture, place a sheet of paper. Make a sign, asking kids to guess how far each town is from their church. Kids write their names and guesses on each sheet of paper. Kids who get the closest (for each town) win a prize on the last day or during closing program. (You can find out how far each town is by using an online map service such at Google Maps or Mapquest.)

Cowpokes

Fun Days

Enlist the help of VBS children and team members to set the stage for SonWest Roundup. Each day of VBS, ask children and team members to bring in or wear items to enhance the fun. Consider doing one or more of the following:

★ **Hat Day** Children and VBS team members wear fun, funny and fantastic Western hats that they bring from home or that they make at VBS using a variety of art supplies.

★ **Animal Day** Dress up as an animal you might see in a Wild-West town: armadillo, lizard, horse, cow, prairie dog, coyote, vulture, snake, etc. It could be a full costume, T-shirt, face paint or whatever!

★ **Funny Hair Day** Encourage everyone involved in your VBS program to come up with their most outrageous hairstyle.

★ **Color of the Day** Using either the color of your choice or each day's Ultimate Point Pennant as a guide, children and VBS team members wear the color of the day in their clothing or even their hair!

Group Names

Group your children by:

★ **Type of Wild-West Animal** Daring Armadillos, Laughing Lizards, Happy Horses, Kind Cows, Peppy Prairie Dogs, Howling Coyotes, Silly Snakes, Hee-Haw Donkeys, Grinning Bobcats, Happy Javelina, Busy Bison, etc.

★ **Things You Might See at a Wild-West Town:** Kooky Cacti, Sensational Sunsets, Miracle Mesas, Hitching Posts, Loopy Lassos, Stompin' Boots, Silly Saddles, Speedy Stagecoaches, etc.

Photographic Memories

In addition to or instead of the Wild-West Photo suggested on page 32 of this guide (and in Special Events in Folder A **A** on the *Planning Guide CD-ROM*), provide other photo opportunities at Wrangler Roundup, Closing Program or other special events. Other photo opportunities could include the following:

★ Children pose with skit actors dressed as their character (see *Rip-Roarin' Assemblies* for descriptions of skit characters).

★ Children pose in front of SonWest Roundup or other backdrop wearing Western clothing (jeans, cowboy boots, plaid shirts, cowboy hats, etc.). Or find patterns for both preschool- and elementary-sized "cowpoke" photo-op standups in *Wild West Décor & More*, complete with face cutouts.

Use the photos as a way to follow up with unchurched families. After VBS, arrange for volunteers to hand-deliver the photos along with a church brochure that includes Sunday School and worship service times, as well as a description of different ministry groups and contact information. Include a prayer request card which can be completed and mailed back to the church prayer team.

Autograph Day

Assign a day for volunteers and children to wear VBS T-shirts. Provide permanent markers for children, skit actors and volunteers to use when signing each other's VBS T-shirts.

VBS Trading Pins

Put SonWest Stickers (available from Gospel Light) on poster board or craft foam, cut out and glue on pin backs. Use for prizes or have children arriving early at VBS make as a craft. VBS team members can place pins on lanyards and distribute throughout the day. Children wear and trade pins all week.

Class Pictures

Select a different graphic image to represent each class (cowboy hat, cactus, sun, horse, etc.). Place die-cut (or photocopied and cut-out) images on sidewalks to form a path, leading from the welcome area to the place where the class gathers at the start of each day's VBS. Use the same image on name tags, class signs, bandannas, visors, etc. Appropriate clip art images are available in *Wild West Décor & More* and at gospellightvbs.com/sonwest or at myvbsparty.com.

The Golden Cowboy Hat

Use metallic gold spray paint to paint a cowboy hat. Use the Golden Cowboy Hat in one or more of the following ways:

★ **Offering** If you collect an offering at your VBS, use one or more Golden Cowboy Hats and pass them around to collect the offering.

★ **Game** Hide the Golden Cowboy Hat on your church campus. At different locations throughout your campus, hide clues that will lead children from one clue to another, eventually discovering the hat. Or instead, make several paper hats from gold paper. Hide hats throughout campus, on walls, in corners, on tree trunks, etc. When a child spots a Golden Cowboy Hat, they keep it to exchange for a prize.

★ **Award** Distribute Golden Cowboy Hat as a prize to a class at each session's Closing Assembly. You may attach the hat to a long pole so that it can be held up as the class travels around your campus, or children may take turns wearing the Golden Cowboy Hat.

Visitor Recognition

Attach small prizes (Bookmarks, Magnets, SonWest Stickers, etc.) to helium-filled balloons and give one to each visitor and the child who brought them. Throughout the day, team members will be able to recognize visitors by the balloons and welcome them to VBS. Or instead of balloons, consider special buttons or stickers kids can wear on their shirts.

The Name's the Game

With permanent markers, children print their names on bandannas and add other decorations. Additional decorations might include SonWest Stickers (available from Gospel Light) or other art supplies.

Songbook

Make a songbook for each VBS child to take home as a reminder of SonWest Roundup. Include the words from the SonWest songs as well as other favorite songs.

SonWest Trading Post

Near your welcome center and/or the place where parents pick up children, place a decorated table and a sign that designates the area as the "SonWest Trading Post." Include for sale several of the prizes and other fun items available from Gospel Light. Parents purchase items for their children as souvenirs of SonWest Roundup.

If you are at a church where there is not a lot of disposable income for souvenirs, consider a "Free Stuff" table. Fill it daily with items that are free for the taking. They could be theme-related items or other small items that have been donated: small toys, books, individually wrapped candies, small articles of clothing, etc.

Guessing Game

In your gathering area or assembly room, prominently display a large transparent container filled with a huge number of small items (marbles, jelly beans, etc.). Or make it theme-related and fill container with small rocks painted gold to look like gold nuggets. Kids guess the number of items in the container to win prizes.

SonWest Roundup on the Town

After VBS, dedicate a bulletin board or post a large sheet of butcher paper in a public area and ask kids to bring in pictures of themselves wearing their SonWest T-shirts in various places: around town, at the beach, on vacation, at school, etc. Keep it going year-round! With parent permission, the photos could be on a page of your church's website or in a newsletter. Send SonWest T-shirts to the children of missionaries your church sponsors and ask them to send in their pictures, too!

Wild-West Workers

Team Names

- ★ **Marshall (Bill):** Director
- ★ **Deputy (Donna):** Activity Center Leaders, Guides
- ★ **Ranch Hands:** Adult and Youth Helpers

Countdown

In your church bulletin and/or in the lobby of your church or other public area, provide a countdown beginning 10 weeks prior to your VBS: "Only 72 more days until SonWest Roundup begins!" Each week update the countdown.

Dedication Service

Plan to hold a dedication service for VBS workers during a regular worship service. Enlist your pastor's approval and help. Print the names of volunteers in a bulletin insert and/or read names aloud. Volunteers come forward to receive special theme-related name tags (available from Gospel Light) and then stand while the pastor prays for them. Consider serving theme-related snacks after the service.

Dress the Part

Encourage your VBS team to dress appropriately for the Wild-West theme, wearing Western shirts, jeans, suede vests, bolo ties, cowboy boots, etc. Before VBS begins, consider buying matching shirts for all volunteers as uniforms. Host a time for team members to decorate straw cowboy hats for the Wild-West theme. Team members use a hot glue gun to glue toy animals, plastic lizards, feathers, beads, leather lacing, bandannas and other appropriately themed craft supplies to their hats.

Prayer Box

Decorate a box with images from *Wild West Décor & More,* SonWest Stickers or other images. Place in the team break room. Keep slips of paper and pencils or pens next to box so that team members can write down prayer requests and place in box. Each day, share requests at your volunteer meeting and then refer requests to your VBS prayer team.

Ask Me!

Prior to VBS, print up stickers or make buttons for volunteers to wear to church activities that read, "Ask me about SonWest Roundup." Also try, "I'll be at SonWest Roundup. How about you?" or "I'm EXCITED about SonWest Roundup!" Use logo or other art from *Wild West Décor & More*, gospellightvbs.com or myvbsparty.com. Don't forget to add the dates and times for your VBS.

Wild-West Characters

Ask skit actors and other volunteers who work behind the scenes to dress in theme-related clothing and greet children as they arrive at each center and/or participate in activities with children.

VBS Mascot

Consider a mascot who returns each year. Even if this mascot is an adult in an animal costume, they can dress in theme-related clothing and lead different segments of the assemblies, participate in various activities and interact with kids throughout VBS. Year after year, kids will look forward to the return of this character.

Snack Attack

Show your VBS team that they are appreciated with a special lounge in which they can take their breaks, talk with each other, pray together and enjoy snacks prepared especially for them. Consider asking the parents of your VBS children to donate snacks. Provide a variety of sweet and salty items along with beverages. Be sure to offer treats reminiscent of a Western town: chili, root-beer floats, hot dogs—and plenty of COFFEE!

Volunteer Newsletter

Use the Volunteer Newsletters in Folder C 📁 on the *Planning Guide CD-ROM* to create a daily newsletter for your VBS team members. Customize the newsletters with important announcements, contact names and numbers, revised schedules or other changes, as well as anecdotes and/or photos from the previous day's activities. Distribute the newsletters at morning team devotional time, place them in the team break area or send them via e-mail the night before each session.

How to Lead the Theme Center

The Theme Center Activities in Folder B on the Planning Guide CD-ROM are designed to give your children the fun of adventures at a Western town, while helping them understand how the biblical focus of each session applies to their own lives.

Display children's work in your classroom. Parents will enjoy viewing their children's work as part of your Closing Program.

Note: The Theme Center Activities are written for children in grades 3 and 4. Adaptation ideas for children in grades 1 and 2 and grades 5 and 6 are included where appropriate. Please use the suggested adaptations to keep activities and conversation age appropriate.

Theme Center Basics

Either by yourself or with another teacher or helper, complete the following steps:

1. Familiarize yourself with each session's overview. Read the Bible Story references, Story Recap, Bible Verse and Jesus Connection so that you can easily talk about them with the children. Memorize the Jesus Connection so that you can guide conversation with your children toward this learning objective.

2. For each session, review the Goals for Each Child. These aims are primarily met in the Bible Story Center; however, one or more of these learning objectives will be met by each Theme Center activity. (Note: Only goals for grades 3 and 4 have been included in the Theme Center Activities. Goals for grades 1 and 2 and grades 5 and 6 differ slightly and are available in *Saddle Up! Bible Stories* for those age levels.)

3. Collect supplies or submit a list to your VBS Director or Supply Coordinator. Group general supplies together and place supplies specific to each day in a labeled box or bag. Prepare items as needed.

4. Shortly before VBS, decorate your assigned classroom (see Sights & Sounds on p. 21. For more decorating ideas and patterns see *Wild West Décor & More*).

5. During VBS, prepare for each session by reading the Heart Prep. Then check to make sure you have the needed materials. Review the instructions until you feel confident leading children in the activities.

6. Lead children in the activity. Use the conversation suggestions provided to help children understand the Bible truths and discover how those truths apply to their everyday lives. In your discussion, be alert for natural openings to talk with children about the wonderful opportunity they have to receive God's love and forgiveness and become members of His family. (See Leading a Child to Christ in Folder B on the *Planning Guide CD-ROM*.)

7. After each VBS session, review the questions provided in Daily Recap. Answer the questions honestly and plan ways to make your next session even better.

26

Theme Center Activities

Session 1: 'Dillo Drawing

Follow simple instructions for drawing an armadillo.

Session 2: Lizard Food

Make a sweet treat that looks like a lizard.

Session 3: Western Relay

Run a Western-inspired relay race.

> These ideas are explained in detail in Theme Center Activities in Folder B **B** on the *Planning Guide CD-ROM*. Read this article to find a list of materials, preparation instructions and detailed steps for each of the activities described here.

Session 4: Udderly Amazing!

Milk a pretend cow and make REAL butter to eat.

Session 5: Pop-Up Prairie Dogs

Make prairie-dog pop-up toys and play a target game.

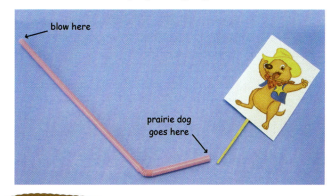

blow here

prairie dog goes here

SPECIAL EVENTS

Imagine the impact special events can have on your church and community. Special events pump up the fun and enthusiasm associated with VBS, whether the events occur before, during or after VBS! Special events give your children unique opportunities to deepen relationships and apply what they are learning about God and the life-changing truths we find in His Word. Add a day, a week or a summer of fun to your SonWest Roundup experience. The effect it will have on the lives of kids and in your community will be well worth it!

Field Trips

Before taking groups of children away from church property, be sure to have parents complete and sign permission and medical-release forms similar to those in Folder C **C** on the *Planning Guide CD-ROM*.

★ **Campfire Tales** Arrange an evening family gathering at a local park or campground. After a simple meal of Western-inspired food like hot dogs and beans, gather everyone around a campfire to sing cowboy or western songs. As the fire dies down, listen to a professional storyteller tell tales of the Wild West.

★ **Western Town** Head off to a nearby Western-themed restaurant, store or tourist location, preferably one with activities in which the children can participate. Take photos of children and when pictures have been printed, send to children as a keepsake. Or with permission, post the photos on your church's website.

★ **Golden Saddle Revue** Invite families to the grand opening of SonWest's Golden Saddle Theater, where they can participate in a talent show. The music leader and team can preview SonWest songs in between acts performed by the children and families in attendance. Serve some of the "Saddle-Up Snacks" (p. 32) during Intermission.

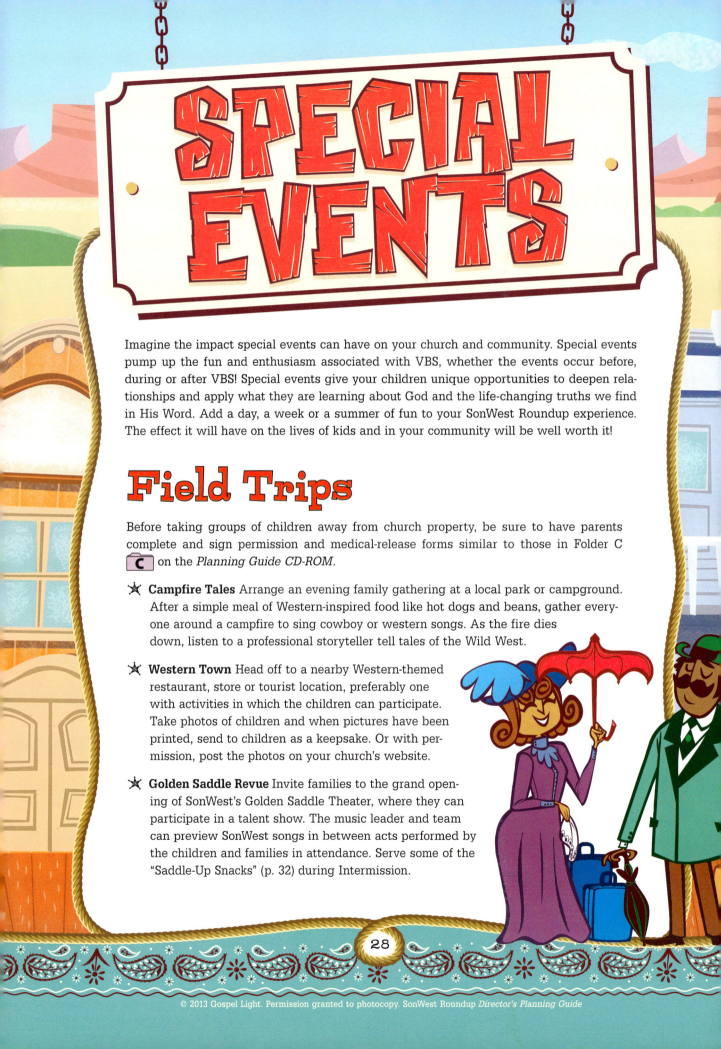

28

Closing Program

The Closing Program is the culmination of your entire VBS program. It may also be your best opportunity for forming relationships with parents of unchurched children. The program is designed to recap the fun events of VBS as well as present the plan of salvation, giving children and their families the opportunity to hear and respond to the good news of Jesus Christ. Make this event one your children, their parents and your team members will long remember!

Read Closing Program in *Rip-Roarin' Assemblies* and on Folder B 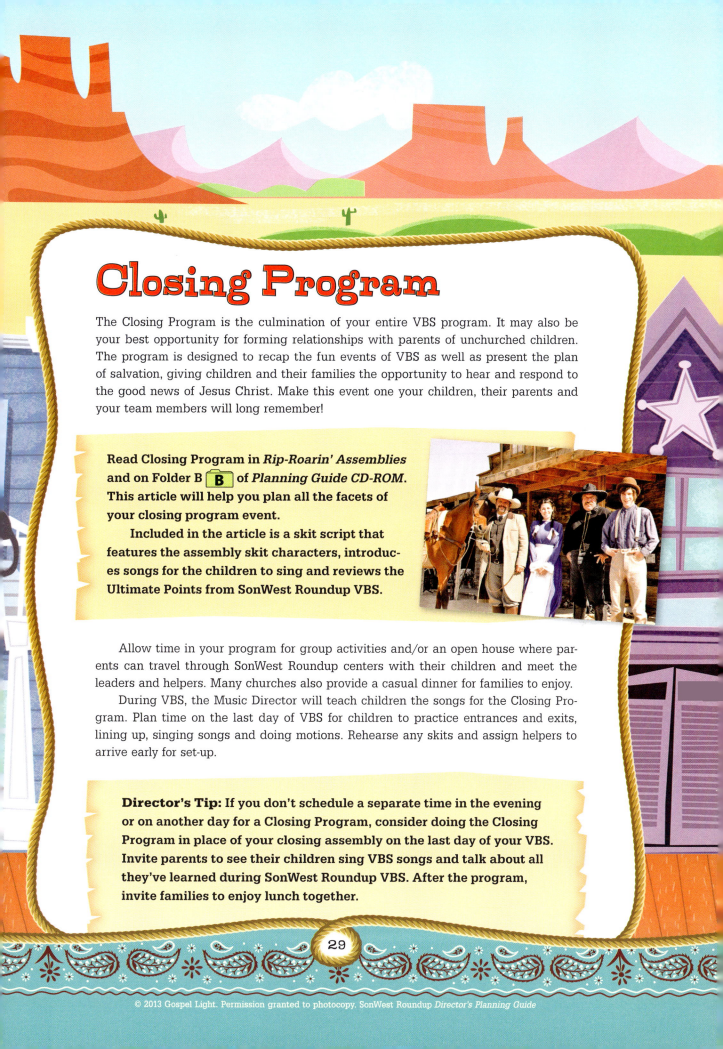 **of *Planning Guide CD-ROM*. This article will help you plan all the facets of your closing program event.**

Included in the article is a skit script that features the assembly skit characters, introduces songs for the children to sing and reviews the Ultimate Points from SonWest Roundup VBS.

Allow time in your program for group activities and/or an open house where parents can travel through SonWest Roundup centers with their children and meet the leaders and helpers. Many churches also provide a casual dinner for families to enjoy.

During VBS, the Music Director will teach children the songs for the Closing Program. Plan time on the last day of VBS for children to practice entrances and exits, lining up, singing songs and doing motions. Rehearse any skits and assign helpers to arrive early for set-up.

Director's Tip: If you don't schedule a separate time in the evening or on another day for a Closing Program, consider doing the Closing Program in place of your closing assembly on the last day of your VBS. Invite parents to see their children sing VBS songs and talk about all they've learned during SonWest Roundup VBS. After the program, invite families to enjoy lunch together.

Events at Church

★ **Cowboy Movie Night** Invite VBS families and post flyers around your town to advertise an evening showing at your church of a Western movie appropriate for all ages. Build a campfire and rent equipment to project the movie on a large wall while everyone sits in camp chairs or on blankets. Provide snacks and information about your church's children's programs.

★ **Western Crafting** Choose one or more of the craft projects from *Trading Post Crafts for Kids*. Set aside a day or evening to make the project. Break up your time by gathering for a few minutes of singing VBS songs and having a snack

(see p. 32 or *Miss Sheryl's Snack Cards*). Invite your pastor or another leader to dress in theme-related clothing and read aloud a children's story about the Wild West. Or, if your event is in the evening, consider a campfire over which to cook hot dogs and beans and to roast marshmallows.

★ **Weekly Events** Plan a special event once a week for each of the five weeks before or after VBS. At each event, do a different activity from Theme Center Activities in Folder B **B** of the *Planning Guide CD-ROM*.

★ **Serving Together** At an all-church gathering, divide the group into intergenerational teams of six to ten people. Ask each team to come up with a team name and provide team name tags for them to decorate. Serve snacks made from recipes in *Miss Sheryl's Snack Cards* or other favorite recipes. Teams brainstorm and plan a project they can do to serve their church family: picking up papers left in sanctuary after church services, helping with landscaping, picking up trash on church campus, sending thank-you notes to pastors and Sunday School teachers, serving as a welcome team to greet visitors, etc. Teams come back together and share their plans.

★ **Summer Program** Keep the spirit of VBS alive all summer long with the program designed to go along with SonWest Roundup: *Wrangler Roundup*, a 13-lesson adventure for children ages 3-12. *Wrangler Roundup* packs the fun and excitement

of a Wild-West town with the discovery of the ULTIMATE gifts Jesus provides for members of God's family. Through engaging Bible stories about Moses, music and activities, children will develop an awareness and confidence in their relationship with Jesus. Use this course as a second-hour program on Sundays, a midweek evening program or any time you work with kids. You and your students will enjoy the flexible format and the variety of activities offered. *Wrangler Roundup* is available from Gospel Light.

★ **SonWest Reunion** After VBS, plan a one-day VBS reunion to keep in contact with new kids who came to VBS. For snack and activity ideas, see the suggestions on pages 32-33. Also consider bringing back games and activities that were popular with children during VBS. Use this event as an opportunity to build relationships with unchurched children and their families. Be ready to invite them to other family programs at your church.

Whether as a preview event to build enthusiasm and register kids for VBS, or as a Fall kickoff, this event is a great opportunity to reach out to children and families in your community.

Promote your event through your church website and e-mail invitations. Reach families who have never attended an event at your church by placing large signs on the streets near your church. Take one evening a few weeks before the event to have groups hang door hangers or knock on doors to hand out flyers to the families in neighborhood homes.

At the event, be sure to give information about your regular ministries and upcoming special events. Be sure to have plenty of registration materials and flyers to give to families. Ask attendees to sign a registration book, and use the contact information to mail or hand-deliver brochures to the families.

Your primary goal at this event is to motivate parents and children to enroll in your upcoming VBS program. Schedule your event two to four weeks before VBS.

Later in the summer, sponsor a Fall Kickoff for the families in your church, the unchurched children who attended VBS as well as kids who have never attended an event at your church before. The informal atmosphere at this event will help welcome them to your church.

Read the information below in Event Staffing, Registration and Information Booth, Event Setup, Saddle-Up Snacks and Giddy-Up Activities for helpful tips and a variety of snack and activity ideas from which to choose. There are enough suggestions to host a preview event AND a Fall Kickoff!

Event Staffing

✸ Each activity needs at least one adult or youth helper to be in charge. Encourage helpers to dress in theme-related clothing.

✸ Ask individual families or adult Sunday School classes or small groups in your church to organize a booth for the Wrangler Roundup.

✸ Have several helpers and/or the skit characters greet parents and encourage children to try any activity that is low on participation.

Registration and Information Booth

Set up a tent or table near the entrance to the Wrangler Roundup. At this site, parents may register their children for VBS or other ministry events.

Give each child a copy of the Wrangler Roundup Pass that will allow them to participate in all activities and receive both refreshments and a small gift (such as a button to wear). When children participate in an activity, they get their passes punched or receive a sticker on the space marked for that activity.

Note: This pass can also be given out in advance at Sunday School, a park, a local business or door-to-door, etc., to promote your event.

Wrangler Roundup Pass

A modifiable version of Wrangler Roundup Pass is in Folder C **C** on the *Planning Guide CD-ROM*.

Event Setup

Transform your church parking lot, lawn or indoor all-purpose room into a fun Western adventure party with games, activities and snacks. Designate each activity area with colored chalk; an awning, stakes and rope; or even booths. Tents and awnings can be used for appropriate activities. Add a thematic touch by using bright paints and fabrics, or paint Western scenes and animals on structures.

Party rental companies often carry a number of activities suited for such a fun event. You can rent inflatables such as ball and bounce houses, funny mirrors, coin-operated rides, rock-climbing walls, kiddie trains as well as carnival-type rides. And don't forget snow-cone machines and popcorn carts! Contact your local supplier and make decisions based on your facility and budget.

Saddle-Up Snacks

Open easy-up tents to cover several tables and chairs or spread tablecloths out on a grassy area on which people can picnic. Cover serving tables with checkered tablecloths. Serve some or all of the following snacks and drinks:

Dusty Popcorn
Provide buttered popcorn and a bowl of cinnamon-sugar with a teaspoon. Children place a cup of popcorn and spoonful of cinnamon-sugar into a paper bag and shake before eating.

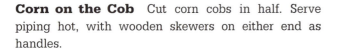

Corn on the Cob Cut corn cobs in half. Serve piping hot, with wooden skewers on either end as handles.

Chuck Wagon Chili Serve canned or homemade chili topped with grated cheese.

Cowboy Sushi Spread a thin layer of cream cheese over a thinly sliced piece of deli meat. Wrap around a dill pickle. Repeat, until pickle has four layers of cream cheese and meat. Slice the pickle into thick slices and serve cold.

Campfire Dogs Serve barbequed hot dogs on a wooden skewer. No buns needed!

Lip-Smackin' Lemonade Serve lemonade in plastic or paper cups. You may also want to provide juicers, sugar, water and lemon halves so that children can try making their own lemonade.

Homemade Ice Cream For added fun, use a hand-crank freezer and let the children do the cranking. Provide a variety of toppings for folks to make sundaes their own way.

Hay Bales In a large saucepan, melt 3 tbsp butter or margarine over low heat. Add a 10-oz. package of marshmallows and stir until marshmallows are melted. Remove pan from heat and add 6 cups puffed-rice cereal. Stir to coat cereal well. Use a buttered spatula to spread mixture into a 13x9-inch (33x23-cm) pan coated with nonstick spray. When cool, cut into rectangles.

Giddy-Up Activities

In addition to the ideas below, consider using some of the activities suggested in Theme Center Activities in Folder B **B** on the *Planning Guide CD-ROM.*

Before your event, use a computer to create a map of your facility showing the locations of the different activities, snacks, bathrooms, assembly rooms, etc.

Wild-West Photo On a large piece of cardboard, paint a Western scene. Place an inflatable cactus next to the scene. Patterns and other scenery ideas are available in *Wild West Décor & More.* Cut out pictures of animals and attach to scene. Or use adhesive spray to attach pictures to foam board before cutting out to make large free-standing cutouts. Arrange cutouts in front of scene. Kids wear SonWest T-shirts, cowboy boots, bandannas and other Western clothing and pose for photographs in front of scenery. Provide additional props such as hay bales, lassos, lanterns, saddles, plastic lizards and stuffed animals for children to pose with as their picture is taken. (SonWest Photo Frame available from Gospel Light.)

Smithing Tin Use nails and hammers to punch holes into pie tins to make words and designs.

Wood Burning Set up an area with wood and wood-burning tools. Older children write their names or create designs on wood. Attach a picture hanger to back of each wood project.

Leather Work Set up an area with leather supplies and tools. Children can tool, braid or paint leather to make leather into wristbands or bookmarks.

Boot Toss Use rope or chalk to make a starting line. Set up several barrels or crates at a variety of distances from the starting line. Young children face barrels and toss boots into them. For an added challenge, older children bend over and toss the boots between their legs, into the barrels.

SonWest Gold Panning Spray-paint small rocks gold or purchase gold aquarium gravel. Pour "gold" nuggets into a large plastic tub and cover with several inches of sand and water. Children scoop up mixture with pie tins and then swirl and tip pans back and forth until everything flows out except for gold nuggets. Add water as needed. Children can exchange gold nuggets for small prizes (stickers, individually wrapped candies, etc.).

Old-Fashioned Races Set up an area for races. Provide burlap sacks for sack races and bandannas to tie two participants together for three-legged races.

SonWest Roundup Skits Have the assembly skit characters greet guests and perform parts of the assembly skits (see *Rip-Roarin' Assemblies*) or skits you have created especially for this event.

Set aside a place for kids to get autographs from the skit characters, other kids and VBS team members. Consider having kids staple or otherwise bind together SonWest Postcards (available from Gospel Light) to form an autograph book.

Ride 'Em, Cowboy Arrange to have a horse or pony at your roundup. Children take turns donning a cowboy hat and taking a ride on the horse or pony.

Train Depot Use chalk or tape to draw a meandering train track in an open area. Hook together several children's wagons and have an adult pull the front "engine" along the track to give younger kids a fun train ride.

NURSERY & TODDLER

Providing child care for your volunteers during meetings and at VBS is an extremely important issue in recruiting. Parents will want the very best care for their own children while they are volunteering to work with the children of others.

Choosing Caregivers

If you expect to have quite a few children in the nursery/toddler age range, consider asking an experienced volunteer to be your Nursery & Toddler Coordinator. This person will be responsible for creating a safe and interesting environment with age-appropriate activities and should assist in recruiting other caregivers to serve.

You will need at least one caregiver for every two babies or every three toddlers. Always plan for at least two caregivers in the nursery, no matter how few children are present.

> **If you have a Nursery & Toddler Coordinator at your church, give them this guide, the Nursery Schedule from Folder C** `C` **on the** *Planning Guide CD-ROM*, **as well as these articles from Folder B** `B` **:** **Playtime with Babies & Toddlers and Planning Your Preschool VBS.**

Teaching Babies & Toddlers

✸ This guide provides a session outline for each day of VBS. Because young children learn well through repetition, there is one Bible verse for all five sessions. Each day's Bible story may be told or read from the big books from *Pony Corral Posters & Props*. There are also two learning activities suggested for each session. Activities may need to be modified. For instance, instead of gluing items to a paper, children simply color the paper.

✸ *Pony Corral Posters & Props* includes attractive posters to use in decorating. Also, decorating ideas are in Planning Your Preschool VBS in Folder B `B` on the *Planning Guide CD-ROM*. Babies and toddlers will also enjoy listening to the music on the *Music & More CD* or watching the videos of the preschool songs from the *Music Leader DVD*.

✸ Read Playtime for Babies & Toddlers `B`. This article is jammed full of great ideas for teaching and playing with young children.

✸ For younger toddlers and babies, the activities referred to should be used one-on-one and should continue as long as the child expresses interest. Do not force a child to sit still or participate in any activity in which they are not interested.

34

Planning a Schedule

The goal of this program is to teach individually each baby and toddler through natural learning processes what they can begin to learn about God. Below is a sample VBS nursery schedule for children two to three years old. Follow the schedule loosely and adapt it to fit your needs.

Nursery Schedule

8:30-9:00	Parents sign in and drop off children. Play soft music. Children enjoy independent play.
9:00-9:30	If appropriate, one or two caregivers take three-year-olds into Opening Assembly with other age groups. Children under three years continue independent play.
9:30-9:45	Bible Story. Puppet welcome time. Movement activities (stretching, finger play, copycat, etc.).
9:45-10:30	Bible Learning Activities. Also free play. Children choose their activities.
10:30-10:45	Snack.
10:45-11:15	Outdoor walk and play.
11:15-11:30	Circle Time. Lay a large blanket on the floor and have children sit on it. Bring a picture book (about animals, families, nature, etc.) to look at with children. Sing songs that involve movement with children.
11:30-11:55	Bible Learning Activities. Also free play. Children choose their activities.
11:55-12:00	Free play and cleanup.
12:00-12:15	Parents pick up children.

Bible Story: Exodus 1:1—2:10

Bible Verse: "God so loved the world that he gave his one and only Son." John 3:16

Lesson Focus: God loves us and helps us every day.

Goals for Each Child:

During this session, each child may

1. SHOW motions from a story about when Moses was born;
2. SAY names of children God loves;
3. THANK God for His love and help.

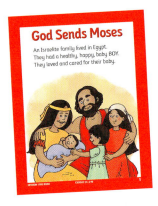

Bible Story

Materials: Bible, "God Sends Moses" Session 1 Big Book from *Pony Corral Posters & Props*

Procedure: Hold up big book so that children can see the pictures as you read or tell the story. Invite children to do appropriate story motions (cradle arms as if holding a baby, shake head "no," etc.).

Bible Learning Activities

Find the Baby

Materials: Bible, baby doll, large basket

Preparation: Hide the baby doll in a place accessible to the children. Place basket in middle of playing area.

Procedure: Children search for the baby doll. Child who finds the baby places it in the basket. Ask children to close their eyes as you hide the baby doll again.

Surprise Tub

Materials: Bible, sensory tub or large plastic storage bin, white packing peanuts, several Christmas story-related items (small unbreakable Christmas ornaments, cotton balls [for sheep], swatches of fake fur, bits of hay, small gold-colored items, etc.)

Preparation: Fill the sensory tub or bin with packing peanuts. Hide Christmas items in the tub or dishpan.

Procedure: **Today we're going to play a game with items that remind us of Christmas!** Children explore the texture of the packing peanuts and search in the tub or bin to find the hidden objects. Invite children to tell what each item is. Tell what part of the Christmas story an item reminds you of. Children hide items back in tub for others to find.

Talk About

★ **The Bible story today tells about when Moses was a baby. To keep baby Moses safe, his mother put him in a basket. Let's look for a baby doll and put it in a basket!**

★ **The story of Moses as a baby reminds me of another story in the Bible. The Bible tells us about when Jesus was born! Every year, we celebrate Jesus' birthday at Christmas.**

★ Hold open Bible. **Our Bible says, "God so loved the world that he gave his one and only Son." God's one and only Son is Jesus! God sent Jesus because He loves us!**

★ **God loves and helps all the people here today. Let's say our names!** Encourage children to say their names aloud. Say the name of any child who cannot speak yet. **God loves us all!**

★ Pray briefly with children. **Dear God, thank You for loving us. Thank You for helping us and sending us Your Son, Jesus. In Jesus' name, amen.**

Bible Story: Exodus 3:1—4:31

Bible Verse: "God so loved the world that he gave his one and only Son." John 3:16

Lesson Focus: God loves us and helps us every day.

Goals for Each Child:

During this session, each child may

1. SHOW motions from a story about a time Moses talked with God;
2. CLAP hands to show we're happy that God loves us;
3. THANK God for His love and help.

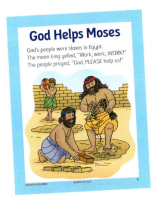

Bible Story

Materials: Bible, "God Helps Moses" Session 2 Big Book from *Posters & Props*

Procedure: Hold up big book so that children can see the pictures as you read or tell the story. Invite children to do appropriate story motions (hold hands as if praying, bend arms to make muscles to show "power," etc.).

Bible Learning Activities

Desert Sandbox

Materials: Bible, bed sheet, items found in the desert (sand, small rocks and stones, bits of dried brush or wood, etc.), one or more large plastic storage bins

Preparation: Place sheet on floor under table to catch sand that falls. Put 1 inch (2.5 cm) of sand in each storage bin.

Procedure: Children observe and touch desert items and then play with items in the sand. Briefly tell about the desert where Moses saw the burning bush.

Texture Walk

Materials: Bible, variety of materials with different textures (cardboard, velvet fabrics, plastic placemats, carpet squares, towels, bubble wrap, newspapers, sandpapers, etc.)

Preparation: Arrange the different materials to create a path through the room. (Older children may help arrange the path.)

Procedure: **In our Bible story today, Moses took off his sandals because God told him to. Let's take off our shoes and socks to walk on our path.** Children remove their shoes and socks and walk on the path you created. Talk with children about how each material feels.

Talk About

★ The Bible story today tells us about a time Moses saw a burning bush. God talked to Moses. God had an important job for Moses to do! God wanted Moses to help His people.

★ Because God loves us, He sent Jesus to help us. Let's jump up and down and clap our hands to show we're glad God loves and helps us. Encourage children to jump and clap with you.

★ Hold open Bible. The Bible says, "God so loved the world that he gave his one and only Son." Sending Jesus is one way that God showed how much He loves us and will help us.

★ Pray briefly with children. Dear God, thank You for loving us. Thank You for sending Jesus and for always helping us. In Jesus' name, amen.

Bible Story: Exodus 5:1—12:51

Bible Verse: "God so loved the world that he gave his one and only Son." John 3:16

Lesson Focus: God loves us and helps us every day.

Goals for Each Child:

During this session, each child may

1. SHOW motions from a story about how God rescued His people from Egypt;
2. SING songs of thanks to God;
3. THANK God for His love and help.

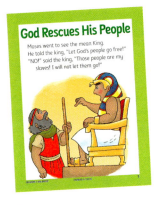

Bible Story

Materials: Bible, "God Rescues His People" Session 3 Big Book from *Posters & Props*

Procedure: Hold up big book so that children can see the pictures as you read or tell the story. Invite children to do appropriate story motions (point finger as if asking to go away, shake head "no," etc.).

Bible Learning Activities

Frogs A-Jumpin'

Materials: Bible, several sheets of green construction paper for each child; Optional—construction paper frogs (laminated, if possible)

Procedure: **In today's Bible story, we heard how God sent hundreds and thousands of FROGS to Egypt. Let's pretend we're frogs!** Children place their green papers on the ground and hop or step over them. After jumping, children pick up the papers and start over. (Optional: Children jump over paper frogs.)

Passover Praise Parade

Materials: Bible, *Music & More CD* and player

Procedure: Play "SonWest Roundup," "God So Loved" and/or "Choosing." Encourage children to join you in walking around the room to the beat of the music. Clap in time to the music as you walk.

As you talk about the Bible story, mention how God's people must have thanked God for sending Moses to help them. Tell the children that singing songs to God is one way we can thank Him for loving us and for giving us the things we need.

Talk About

✷ The Bible story today tells about when God's people left Egypt. In Egypt, God's people had to work hard. The mean king was so unkind to them. The people were so sad!

✷ God loved His people and He cared that they were so sad. God rescued His people from Egypt. God's people were very happy!

✷ Hold open Bible. **The Bible says, "God so loved the world that he gave his one and only Son." God loves us and gives us what we need. And we all need Jesus!**

✷ Pray briefly with children. **Dear God, thank You for loving us and giving us what we need. Thank You for giving us Jesus. We love You! In Jesus' name, amen.**

Session 4:
God Feeds His People

Ultimate TRUST

Bible Story: Exodus 16:1—17:7

Bible Verse: "God so loved the world that he gave his one and only Son." John 3:16

Lesson Focus: God loves us and helps us every day.

Goals for Each Child:
During this session, each child may
1. SHOW motions from a story about how God fed His people;
2. POINT to people God loves;
3. THANK God for His love and help.

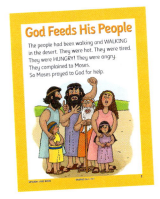

Bible Story

Materials: Bible, "God Feeds His People" Session 4 Big Book from *Posters & Props*

Procedure: Hold up big book so that children can see the pictures as you read or tell the story. Invite children to do appropriate story motions (walk in place, rub stomach as if hungry, etc.).

Bible Learning Activities

Grocery Getters

Materials: Bible, variety of empty grocery containers (cereal boxes, soda bottles, frozen food boxes, etc.), brown grocery bag

Procedure: Volunteers tell what kind of food comes in each grocery container. Then invite a child to predict how many of the containers can be placed into the bag. Each child takes a turn to place a container into the bag until the bag is full. Lead children in counting the items as you remove them from the bag. Continue the activity, testing several additional predictions.

Yummy in the Tummy

Materials: Bible, discarded magazines, scissors, paper plates, glue, crayons or markers

Preparation: Cut out a variety of pictures of food from magazines, at least three pictures for each child.

Procedure: Each child looks through food pictures and glues two or three pictures onto a paper plate. Invite each child to tell what their favorite food is as you write on their plate, "(Chandler) thanks God for (animal crackers)."

Talk About

★ Today's Bible story today tells us how God fed His people when they were hungry. God fed His people because He loved them. He wanted them to have what they needed.

★ God loves us, too! God wants us to have what's best for us, too. That's why God sent us Jesus. God knows what's best for us. Every day, He gives us what we need.

★ God loves . . . Name each child, pointing to them. Encourage children to point with you and say names. Then, ask children to tell you their favorite foods. **God loves you, Isabel! That's why He gives you good food to eat.**

★ Pray briefly with children. **Dear God, thank You for loving us. Thank You for giving us what we need every day. In Jesus' name, amen.**

Bible Story: Exodus 19:1—20:21; 24:12; 25:10-22

Bible Verse: "God so loved the world that he gave his one and only Son." John 3:16

Lesson Focus: God loves us and helps us every day.

Goals for Each Child:

During this session, each child may

1. SHOW motions from a story about how God gave His people rules for showing love;
2. TELL ways God shows His love;
3. THANK God for His love and help.

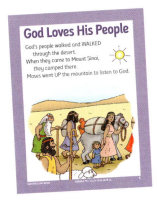

Bible Story

Materials: Bible, "God Loves His People" Session 5 Big Book from *Posters & Props*

Procedure: Hold up big book so that children can see the pictures as you read or tell the story. Invite children to perform appropriate story motions (walk in place, pretend Earth is shaking, etc.).

Bible Learning Activities

Border Walk

Materials: Bible, masking tape

Preparation: Before class, make a masking-tape line that turns several times on the floor of your room. (Remove tape after session.)

Procedure: Children follow the line in a variety of ways: walking, crawling, jumping, etc.

Block Camp

Materials: Bible, brown construction paper, blocks, toy people, toy animals

Procedure: Children build a camp by folding brown sheets of construction paper to make tents and arranging blocks to make a tall mountain around the camp. Briefly tell the action of to-day' Bible story. Children use toy people to act out the story.

Talk About

✸ **In our Bible story today, God gave His people rules to follow. The rules told how to show love to God and others.**

✸ **Jesus gave us a new rule. Jesus said to love others.** Jasmine, I saw you hand a block to Kaden. **That was a kind thing to do. Being kind is a way to obey Jesus and show love to others.**

✸ Hold open Bible. **Our Bible says, "God so loved the world that he sent his one and only Son." God loves us so much, He sent Jesus to help us show love to others every day.**

✸ Pray briefly with children. **Dear God, thank You for loving us. Thank You for sending Jesus and helping us show love to others every day. In Jesus' name, amen.**